Why do people bully?

Adam Hibbert

HODDER
Wayland

an imprint of Hodder Children's Books

© 2004 White-Thomson Publishing Ltd

Produced for Hodder Wayland by
White-Thoi
2/3 St Andi
Lewes
BN7 1UP

Other titles in this series:
Why are people racist?
Why are people refugees?
Why are people terrorists?
Why are people vegetarian?
Why do families break up?
Why do people abuse human rights?
Why do people commit crime?
Why do people drink alcohol?
Why do people fight wars?
Why do people gamble?
Why do people harm animals?
Why do people join gangs?
Why do people live on the streets?
Why do people smoke?
Why do people take drugs?

Editor: Philip de Ste. Croix
Cover design: Hodder Children's Books
Inside design: Malcolm Walker
Consultant: Dr. Kenneth Rigby, Adjunct Associate
  Professor of Social Psychology, University of
  South Australia.
Picture research: Shelley Noronha, Glass Onion
Indexer: Amanda O'Neill

Published in Great Britain in 2004 by Hodder
Wayland, an imprint of Hodder Children's Books

The right of Adam Hibbert to be identified as the
author has been asserted by him in accordance
with the Copyright, Designs and Patents Act 1988.

British Library Cataloguing in Publication Data
Hibbert, Adam, 1968-
  Why do people bully?
  1. Bullying - Juvenile 2. Bullying - Psychological
  aspects - Juvenile literature
  I. Title II. De Ste. Croix, Philip
  371.5'8

ISBN 0 7502 4327 9

Printed by C&C Offset, China

Hodder Children's Books
A division of Hodder Headline Limited
338 Euston Road, London NW1 3BH

Picture acknowledgements
The publisher would like to thank the following
for their kind permission to use their pictures:
Angela Hampton Family Life Picture Library 4, 5, 7,
8, 9, 10, 15, 24, 32, 42; Eye Ubiquitous 21 (Bruno
Zarri), 25 (Paul Seheult), 30 (Paul Seheult), 43 (Paul
Seheult); Getty Image (cover) (David Young-Wolff);
Richard and Sally Greenhill 40; Hodder Wayland
Picture Library (imprint page), (contents) (left), 6,
14, 16, 28, 33, 34, 41; Impact Photos 13 (Robin
Laurence); James Davis Travel Photography 27;
Oxford Scientific Films 20 (Zig Leszczynski);
Photofusion 35 (Paul Baldesare); Popperfoto 12,
37 (middle), 37 (lower) (Reuters/Garry Caskey);
Skjold 29; Topham/ImageWorks 17 (Richard Lord),
(contents) (right), 18, 23 (James Nubile), 26
(Journal-Courier, Steve Warmowski), 38, 39 (Bob
Daemmrich), 45; Topham/PA 44; Topham/Photri 19,
22; Topham Picturepoint 11, 31.

Cover picture: Student sitting alone
in a school corridor. Bullying in schools
is quite a common problem.

Contents

1.What is bullying?

The boundaries of bullying

What do punching someone in the playground and whispering behind someone's back have in common? They may both be called bullying. A wide range of behaviours can be called bullying. Of course, not all aggressive behaviour is bullying. For example, someone may play sports in an aggressive way, or someone may seem aggressive when he or she is sticking up for themselves or a friend. There are several elements that make behaviour an example of bullying.

The first is the issue of power. When two equals argue or fight, we do not call either of them a bully – we see that as a 'fair fight'. Bullying is done by a person with more power to a person with less power. The victim may be chosen because he or she cannot defend themself against the bully at that time.

▼ *In games like soccer, players need to be pushy to gain control of the ball. But that sort of physical aggression is quite different from bullying.*

But that is not the whole story. In some cases we approve of people with more power using it to intervene in other people's lives, against their wishes. For example, think about the work of the police. We expect them to use their powers to stop someone from committing a crime, or from hurting themselves.

Sometimes we agree that it is in everyone's best interests for the powerful to act in this way – that it is a justified use of power. At other times, we disagree – we say that they have abused their power.

Another element of bullying is that quite often the behaviour is repeated. Bullies often return to a person or group they have chosen as a target. Anyone can be rude or thoughtless to another person, but when they repeat the behaviour it may add up to bullying. But it would be wrong to say that all bullying is repeated behaviour – sometimes a single bullying act is very upsetting.

▲ *Being gossiped and whispered about can make a person feel left out and terribly lonely.*

So to define bullying, we can say that it is when one person is unfairly aggressive towards another, and usually, but not always, this will happen repeatedly over a period of time.

case study · case study · case study · case study · case study

'Every time I walk by this kid he punches me, pushes me, makes fun of me, or hurts me in some way. I am younger than him – I'm in the 7th grade and he's in 9th grade. Sometimes I feel like, if I was only in his grade, I could punch him in the face.
I went to a counsellor in my school and talked to her. She gave me a lot of good advice to ignore him, and move away. It works, but only sometimes. You can never let a bully push you around because then it gets into some serious trouble. They only bully you because they have nothing better to do.'
Angelo, 7th grader, Florida, USA

The bullying experience

An important part of what we mean by bullying is that the bully is cruel to the target. When a bully hurts someone, the bully wants to upset that person. The bully will only be satisfied when the target shows that he or she is hurt – for example, by blushing, crying, becoming angry or running away. So to tell if an action is bullying or not, it is important to know not just what happened, but how both sides felt about it.

Bullies may not fully understand that their behaviour is wrong. Though they see that their target is upset, they may feel that it was alright to upset that person. When other people fail to criticize this behaviour, the bully sees this as a sign of approval. He or she may even think of themselves as a leader, punishing only those people the group dislikes.

weblinks

For more information about children's experience of bullying around the world, go to www.waylinks.co.uk/series/why/bully

◀ *Bullies know they are doing something wrong when they steal food or money from someone weaker than themselves.*

In the same way, victims of bullying may not realize that the way they are being treated is wrong. Others may allow or even encourage the bully to attack them. Victims may think this means that everyone hates them – but the people watching are often held back from helping by fear of becoming a target themselves.

So victims may think that everyone would rather they were dead, when in fact only the bully has a problem with them. In rare cases, victims can even interpret cruelty as a sign of caring about them, and treat their bully as a friend.

▲ *Sometimes a group includes one person who is always picked on – and that person can start to expect to be treated badly.*

The feelings of both bullies and their victims are based on a mistaken idea of what is happening. The bully may not even realize that they have upset someone – they may think that their relationship with the victim is normal and healthy. A bully will often claim to be innocent because they truly feel innocent – unless they can be taught to see where they are going wrong, they may think that they have been punished unfairly. At the same time, victims may believe that they deserve the tough treatment, even though they have done nothing wrong.

FACT:
The three behaviours reported as most hurtful by school pupils are:
1. Someone trying to break up a friendship
2. Being ganged up against.
3. Being excluded from a group.
K. Rigby and D. Bagshaw, 'What Hurts?', Children Australia, 2001

Types of bullying

There are three different types of bullying: verbal, physical and indirect bullying. Verbal teasing is the most common type and is used by both boys and girls. Boys are more likely than girls to use physical force, or the threat of force. Girls prefer to use indirect bullying, such as excluding someone from a group, or other sorts of mental torment.

Almost all young people are teased or called names at some stage in their childhood. Verbal bullying may begin as random teasing, but it can soon become a painful experience for anyone who shows signs of being upset by the names they are called. They may then find themselves the target of nasty jokes, insults and other types of bullying.

▲ Girls tend to be more likely to use non-physical types of bullying, such as name-calling, insults and verbal teasing.

Physical bullying ranges from the threat of pain, to shoving, hitting, hair-pulling and, in some rare cases, severe beatings. It is the most obvious type of bullying for an adult to see and stop. In the past boys were more likely to use physical bullying than girls, but in recent years girls have also started to do this more often.

weblinks

For more information about how to recognize if someone is being bullied, go to www.waylinks.co.uk/ series/why/bully

```
case study · case study · case study · case study · case study
```

'People [at my new school] were OK at first, but then I started to gain weight. People started bugging me about it. I wasn't going to go back to hating myself again. So I was with some kids I thought I wanted to be friends with and they started to pick on this kid. He was minding his own business, wasn't even looking around and they just pounced on him. To fit in I started to insult him too and believe me I'm not complimenting myself, but I was good. So day after day I picked on this kid so people wouldn't pick on me. I messed with his mind. I made him question everything he did. This kid hated me so much. If he could have killed me, I'm sure he would have. I put this kid through four years of hell and I didn't even care.'

Nicholas, victim of bullying – and bully

The indirect bully spreads lies or rumours about a person, and encourages other people to be mean to their victim. Bullies may try to show the victim that they are not wanted, by cutting them out of friendly activities and excluding them from a group. Indirect bullying also includes trying to persuade their friends to turn against them.

◀ *Boys are more likely than girls to use physical power and threats to bully someone.*

Bullying over time

Just as bullying is not one simple thing, the people involved in a bullying relationship are not simply bullies or victims for the rest of their lives. Very young children often experiment with force or name-calling, but this does not mean they will always be bullies. In fact, the younger a child, the more likely it is that their behaviour can be corrected, by their peers as well as by adults.

Bullying behaviour can be a stage that young people go through at some point in their childhood, as they discover new things about themselves and those around them. The same goes for targets of bullying. Most children will be picked on from time to time, which may prompt them to find new ways to stick up for themselves.

▼ *These four-year-olds may be mean to each other accidentally – most soon learn to be nice and to play together as part of a group.*

Film star Harrison Ford, starring here as action hero Indiana Jones, was bullied when he was a child.

But bullying can also reinforce a child's fears, making them more likely to be picked on in the future.

Some research suggests that bullies and targets of bullying have quite a lot in common. Though the evidence is mixed, bullies may be more likely than other people to have also had the experience of being bullied. Experts talk about 'bully/victims' – people who have both experiences, often at different times as they grow up. One explanation for this link may be that both bullies and victims are more worried than other people about not fitting in with a group. Being a bully or being vulnerable to bullying may result from just the same fears.

> 'I was kind of a runty kid. The boys would get together and throw me over the edge of the parking lot into the weeds every day at recess.'
> *Harrison Ford, film star*

2. When does bullying happen?

Bullies in history

The English word 'bully' probably came from the Dutch word for 'brother'. In Shakespeare's plays it is a positive term – in a play about the English king Henry V, one of his soldiers describes him as a 'lovely bully'. In *The Merry Wives of Windsor*, another Shakespeare play, a character getting ready to fight is greeted with the words 'Bless thee, bully doctor!'. It seems to have meant that he was a bold, fearless friend. In the USA, 'bully' survived into the twentieth century as a slang word, like 'cool', for something that was good.

weblinks

For more information about the way the word 'bully' has changed over time, go to www.waylinks.co.uk/series/why/bully

◀ *Shakespeare used the word 'bully' to describe the heroic warrior, King Henry V, here being played by film actor Laurence Olivier.*

Military recruits are in the power of the people who train them. Sometimes the methods used can be very harsh. We might describe them as bullying.

Over time, though, the word took on another darker meaning. By the eighteenth century, calling someone a bully suggested that they were big and brave on the outside, but a coward underneath. Around this time, it began to be used to describe people who abused their power to victimize the weak. By the start of the twentieth century, being called a bully was a bad thing. It simply meant someone who was rude, violent and probably a coward.

In the last 40 years, the modern meaning of the word has changed very slightly. Up until the 1970s, bullies were typically seen as stupid people with whom the rest of us just had to cope. But since then, we have begun to take bullying – and the harm it may do to others – more seriously. In particular, schools have made changes to the way they organize their pupils, to make sure they are not encouraging bullying. 'Bully' now means someone who is quite dangerous and threatening.

> 'Bullying has been part of school life for generations but [it] cannot be tolerated. The victims are emotionally traumatized and can be driven from school. In the worst cases, bullying can lead to suicide. The bullies will graduate on to domestic violence and assault if not confronted. If we are to become a less violent society, we need to start in the playground.'
> *Nick Smith, New Zealand Education Minister*

A learning process

As infants begin to be able to speak and walk, they become more aware of other people, especially other children. From this earliest age, children experiment with how to interact with other people in a group, exploring what it is to live in a society of people.

Part of the problem they have to solve is how to understand who someone else is. They cannot really understand much about their parents at this stage, but other pre-schoolers look like them, and seem to have similar needs and wants. They can begin to make guesses about other children – how they might react to things the child does and choices the child makes, such as sharing a toy or taking it away.

◄ These pre-schoolers are fighting over who will have the bat. They are starting to see how the way they behave affects other people.

At about the same time, toddlers also discover their own independence from their parents, and begin to defend it by using a new word – 'No!'. Testing the boundaries of this freedom can also cause them to be mean to other kids, without there being an obvious reason why they are behaving in this way.

Almost all small children seem to behave like bullies at some point. Most will discover that being assertive gets results, but being anti-social – breaking the rules and being rude to other people – gets them into trouble. Both adults and the children around them will teach them the difference. They begin to work out the rules of good social conduct – and to follow most of them.

▲ *Infants can win attention by crying – this is one way they learn that they can be 'in control' of a situation.*

FACT:

10 per cent of children say they have been bullied by other students, but have not bullied others.

6 per cent say that they have both been bullied, and have bullied other children.

13 per cent of students say they have bullied other students, but have not been bullied themselves.

Journal of the American Medical Association, 25 April 2001

Starting at school

Children's social skills and thought processes are already very complex by the time they first go to school. But younger pupils are less 'streetwise' than children who have been at school for a year or two, so they are easier targets. This may also be the first time that many of them are left to play with others without the presence of grown-ups watching over them. Almost all physical bullying happens at these times.

Unsupervised play is useful for learning. Without an adult to turn to, children have to work out how to deal with conflict and other challenges, such as boredom. Bullying can be triggered by boredom in breaktime – more than half of bullying incidents take place in the last quarter of a breaktime. It is normal for smaller and less experienced children to be the target of 'thrill-seeking' bullies during a dull break period.

▶ *Being the new kid at a school is often a worrying and lonely time.*

The worst time for being singled out occurs during the first year of being at a school – something which happens to most children two or three times in their school careers. Normally, this difficult time passes as 'the new kid' gains a circle of friends and stops being an easy target. But it can make life harder for a child who is forced to move schools, perhaps because a parent takes a job in a different town. For these reasons some schools give support to new pupils by asking an older pupil to look after, or 'mentor', them. This older child's support shows bullies that the smaller kid will not be an easy target.

▲ *Having a circle of friends, hanging out and having fun together shows bullies that a person is not likely to be an easy target.*

```
case study · case study · case study · case study · case study
```

'My family and I move a lot – three times in the past three years. This has taken its toll on my ten-year-old. He is always the new kid. He gets picked on no matter where we go. He is a very smart and loving child. He does not understand the concept of why bullies bully. Everyday it's the same thing. He goes out after school to play and comes back in tears. Sometimes he is so upset that it takes me 20 minutes or so to calm him down.

They are calling him names, taking his toys, taking his bike, kicking his bike, hitting him, kicking him when he is down, and just plain being mean. When new kids move in the neighbourhood my son becomes friends with them until they hook up with the bullies, and then they join the group that picks on my son. I don't know what to do for him. He is such a good kid. My heart breaks when I see the pain this is causing him.'

Michelle, mother of three

Bullying in later life

Recently, some experts have taken what they have learned about bullying in schools in order to study the adult world, especially the workplace. Just as in school, there are people in authority – managers – and a mixed group of workers with their own personalities and goals. Sometimes, the workplace can be a stressful environment , and people can be singled out for harsh treatment.

A 26-year-old postman committed suicide in 1999 after being bullied at work. His employers studied the case, and announced new standards of conduct in 2002. They commented,'basic human decency and respect for everyone working in the organization are at the heart of these standards and a clear message is sent to all employees that anything less will simply not be tolerated.'

weblinks

For more information about bullying in the workplace, go to www.waylinks.co.uk/ series/why/bully

◀ *Managers have to be careful to be fair with every employee, not to abuse their power and bully the weaker members of staff.*

Some military officers bully their trainees and humiliate them in public to make sure that they are totally obedient to the orders they are given.

Bullying in the workplace often involves the relationship between a manager and an employee. This makes it difficult to decide what is acceptable, since part of the job of a manager is to tell an employee what to do. In the past, employees joined trades unions to stand up to managers who were unfair or too demanding. But, as the power of trades unions has declined in recent times, it is now more common for relationships in workplaces to be between individuals one-on-one. Employees feel the stress coming directly from one person, who can easily appear to be a bully.

Bullying is also found where people are paid to look after other people they may not like or respect. Workers at care homes for the elderly or the mentally disabled, and in places such as prisons, are sometimes guilty of bullying people they should be looking after.

3. What are the causes of bullying?

Human nature

Some people argue that bullying is natural; that it is part of human nature. Our nearest animal relations, primates (gorillas, chimps etc.), use force and other bullying tactics to raise their position or status in the group, at the expense of others. And the animal that dominates the group usually fathers more offspring than the others because it has first choice of available mates. So it is possible that nature rewards and encourages bullying.

But it is hard to draw conclusions about human beings from animal examples. Among humans, bullying tends to be associated with low social status – it is seen as a sign that a person is not completely civilized.

◀ *Male chimps pull faces, strike poses and even attack one another to settle who's 'boss' in the group. The leader can choose the females that he will mate with.*

Could a bullying nature be something a child inherits at birth? Studying identical twins can give us some clues to help us decide if genes do play any part in determining how people will behave.

Even when bullies win high social status, there is no evidence that they have more children – there is no biological 'prize' for their achievements. So the genes which drive primate behaviour may not apply to human behaviour. How can we find out?

One way is to study identical twins to see if people with identical genes actually behave in the same way. If one is a bully, will the other be? A study of identical twins in Texas carried out in 1997 gave mixed results – but it suggests that DNA has almost no role in whether a person decides to bully or not.

There is one other fact to consider. Physical bullies are often bigger, stronger and more aggressive than the average person. Not all strong, aggressive people are bullies, but this aspect of bullying is related to a person's genetic 'nature'. We have to think about whether physical strength counts as a 'cause' of bullying, or just gives a person a better 'opportunity' to carry it out.

Home life

Some people argue that it is not human nature that makes bullies, but the way people are brought up or 'nurtured'. Bullying behaviour, they suggest, may be due to problems at home. These problems may be things like bad parenting and violence, or they may be caused by other factors, like poverty.

There is evidence that supports the idea that families in crisis are more likely to produce troubled children. But parents' behaviour is not the whole story. The complete home environment seems to be a factor, as well. Children who live in strong, safe communities with positive adult role models are less likely to be bullies. However, recent research in the United States makes the picture more complicated. Long-term bullies, and victims, seem to come from the whole range of family backgrounds and social classes.

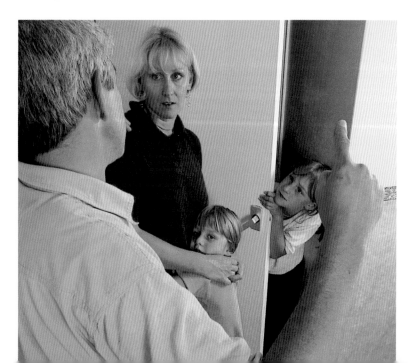

◀ *Children growing up in very unhappy homes may learn to think of feelings of anger and loneliness as being normal.*

Young people may feel less valued when they have to live in dirty, run-down areas. This, in turn, may affect the way that they behave.

But these statistics cannot explain causes; they only show where there are links. For example, if family crisis is more common among the long-term unemployed, is it the family itself or the low social status which causes bad behaviour in the child? Can we be sure that there is no genetic cause that affects both the parent and the child? It is necessary to look at a range of other factors to find causes for each case of bullying.

FACT:
Rates of bullying appear to differ between countries. The best method researchers have found to study bullying is to survey school pupils. But comparing surveys from two different cultural groups is almost impossible. In one study, nearly 80 per cent of German children admitted to having bullied another person in the last term, when in Britain the response was just 22 per cent. Is this because the English word 'bully' means something different from the German word? Is it due to differences between the way of life in Britain and Germany? It just goes to show that this method of research - taking surveys - does not always provide clear-cut answers.

School life

Another powerful influence that affects bullying is the environment in which children spend most of their waking life – with friends and at school. Two schools in the same community can experience very different levels of bullying, according to how they inspire their pupils. Bullying experts have a word for this aspect of a school – 'ethos'. Ethos means the values and spirit set by the school for its pupils.

School ethos may come from the school's traditions, or have something to do with whether it is single-sex or co-ed. It may come from the religious values that are taught there. Girls attending girls-only schools suffer slightly less risk of being bullied, while boys in single-sex schools may suffer slightly more. In co-ed schools, boys bully girls more than girls bully boys, especially by teasing.

weblinks

For more information about the practice of hazing, go to www.waylinks.co.uk/series/why/bully

◀ *Girls are bullied at all-girl schools, but studies show that it is less physical, and happens a bit less often, than it would in co-ed schools.*

Mentors are valuable. When the smallest person at a school is befriended and looked after by the biggest, bullies cannot win.

To understand how important school ethos is to bullying, researchers have to make sure they are not missing something. For example, different sorts of families may choose to send their children to different types of schools – so which comes first, the school ethos or the values that the children bring with them that they have learned in their own families?

Research which takes all these factors into account still finds that big differences in levels of bullying occur between schools. It really does seem to be a matter of school ethos. In some schools, no disrespect is tolerated – in others, the tradition of mobbing or 'hazing' new students is tolerated or even approved of by staff.

'Bullying should not be accepted as a normal part of school life and it must be challenged. Every pupil has the right to expect to be able to learn in a safe environment – and not to be bullied just because they are seen to be a little different.'

David Blunkett, UK Education Secretary, 2000

Individuals and groups

Most people believe that when someone acts like a bully they have made a deliberate choice to behave like this. To prevent bullying, and to help long-term victims of bullying, we have to try to understand what leads someone to make this 'choice'.

◀ Different people respond differently to group activities – some love it, some struggle and find it hard to fit in.

Bullies are often uneasy when asked to take part in group activities. Some lack the social skills to get along with others and earn their respect, so instead they use aggression as a way of getting what they want. Some children may turn to bullying because they are impatient or bored when they have to cooperate with other children. In both cases, bullying comes from a lack of understanding of, or frustration with, social rules – and the response is to be anti-social.

Bullies – and victims – may have experienced an emotional hurt. For example, if parents are suffering a painful marriage or going through a bad divorce, a child may come to think that the adult world is cruel and stupid. They may think that other children with happier home lives are being fooled by adults, or spoiled, and come to resent them.

Different people have different feelings about normal social values like honesty and respect. When bullies and victims are asked about their feelings, both tend to be more critical of such values, perhaps because of their experiences of 'unfair' treatment at school or an unhappy home life. With bullies, the response comes out as frustration and anger, while victims may be picked on because they are uneasy in social situations that other people take for granted.

Feeling odd or left out can make important differences to how a person chooses to look, dress and behave.

27

Looking in the mirror

As children – and as adults – we often think about what sort of person we want to be. Experts call this sense of self 'identity'. We try out different clothes and hairstyles, we copy what we like about other people. We examine people whom we think we resemble to see how they act. We try to get rid of bad habits and weaknesses we think we have found in ourselves. As children, we often rely on fashion and other surface appearances to say 'who' we are.

Children need strong role models in their family, or among other close adults, to help them form this 'identity'. If a child never gets close to an adult who is strong and trustworthy, it can be hard for them to see how to become strong and trustworthy themselves.

Children also need to feel secure with what it means to be a boy or a girl – and they may pick on someone who seems to threaten these roles. Boys quite often use 'girl' as an insult to other boys, for example. The film star Winona Ryder was teased and beaten up by other girls at school for wearing 'boyish' clothes.

▶ *These children are enjoying pretending to be grown-ups. Games like this are a way of exploring their own identities.*

Being a stranger in a new country can make a young person very vulnerable to bullying.

We also build our identity by rejecting things we do not want to be. Often the things that make us angriest about other people are the 'weaknesses' we know that we have too. When boys call each other 'gay', most of the reason is to prove to themselves and others that they are manly. In other words, name-calling often has nothing to do with the target, and everything to do with the bully's own fears about his or her image.

case study · case study · case study · case study · case study

'My name is Sia and I have been to five different schools ever since I came to Canada. My first school was in a little town about a two hours drive from Edmonton where I am living right now. The kids there used to tell me to go back to where I came from and they threw a piece of paper at me … I took it home and I gave the piece of paper to my mom and my mom read it out loud and on that piece of paper it said "black monkey". My mom felt really bad because we just recently came from Africa and we had already started getting problems. The principal at the school dealt with the problem very well. He called down the whole school and spoke to them about what bullying can do to people.'

Sia, Edmonton, Canada

Group loyalties

Groups can help people to fix their own identities. We hang around with a group who all agree on a certain set of values – it might be taste in music, fashion, or some other shared interest. The group's approval of us confirms that our chosen identity is 'working'. There are many positive aspects to this situation. It can give us confidence, seal friendships, teach new skills and let us achieve things we could not do alone.

But there is a negative aspect as well. To establish a group's identity, we sometimes want to reject whatever does not fit. So there can be competition within a group to stay 'near the top' in popularity, as far away as possible from the risk of being rejected by other members of the group.

Fear of rejection may mean that we stand by or do nothing when members of our group criticize or attack others for being different. In schools, the group may include almost the whole school population, with just a few individuals who have been singled out as being different, being rejected. In this way groups can have a bad effect, causing people not to feel any sympathy for others who are being hurt, and making it easier for everyone to avoid blaming themselves for what is happening.

▲ *The boy in the middle is taunting a smaller boy – probably partly in order to impress his friends.*

Groups can also be quite close-knit gangs. In rare cases, the only way to prove that you belong with the gang is to show how nasty you are to outsiders. The leader of this sort of group is typically the one who is the most successful bully – not necessarily a physical bully, but someone who is good at controlling other people.

▶ *Being part of a group can be a very positive experience, but sometimes loyalty to the group can lead to bad consequences – such as bullying people who are not part of the group.*

FACT:

Students, aged 8-18 years, were asked how likely the following outcomes would be if they bullied someone at school. The figures show the percentage (%) of boys and girls that thought an outcome was likely.

	girls	boys
It makes others scared of you	63.1	66.3
I would feel better than the victim	37.7	43.1
I would be ashamed of myself	55.1	42.2
It would show I was tough	31.7	38.0
It would prevent me from being bullied	25.9	33.6
It would get me admired	13.8	21.3
I would feel good about myself	8.5	13.1

K. Rigby, 'Attitudes and beliefs about bullying among Australian school children', 1996

Targets

What about those people who are picked out – is there any one thing about them that triggers people to bully them? The evidence is that bullies usually select targets who are not good at defending themselves. But this is not always the case. Sometimes a bully identifies a target because he or she appears to be a threat.

weblinks

For more information about how to cope with teasing, go to www.waylinks.co.uk/series/why/bully

Many victims of bullying are less assertive, or shyer, than most other people. Shy people are less likely to be able to build a circle of friends to support and defend them. This makes them an easier target for a bully.

The fact that they are less assertive than others also allows a bully to 'project' qualities onto them. For example, if a bully is secretly worried that her friends will discover that she fancies a boy, she might decide to attack another girl for fancying him – just to prove that she thinks those feelings are pathetic. The target may not even know the boy, but the bully guesses that she will not be able to stick up for herself.

▶ *A shy person finds it hard to stand up for herself – so bullies can make up stories about her and make her life a misery.*

Being different from other people, even if it is a simply a matter of being a little overweight, can be a reason for bullies to victimize someone.

Some children are picked on simply for looking different from other children. Ethnic minorities and disabled people are obvious examples, but anything from hair colour to height to weight to style of dress can provide a chance for a bully to pick on another person. If the target seems ashamed or upset, the bully has discovered a weakness to exploit.

case study · case study · case study · case study · case study

'People have been mean to me because I am chubby. At school they call me really horrible names which make me cry. I try not to, but I always do. At home it is just the same. My brothers pick on me because I am younger and shorter than them. My mum tries to make them be nice to me but only one of my brothers ever is. I hate feeling sad all the time and I wish I was thin like all the other kids in my school.

David, aged 9

4.What does bullying do?

Mild cases

Most cases of bullying only last a short time and are quite mild. Children learn, grow and move on every day, and rarely bully – or remain the target of bullying – for a long period. But even short periods of bullying can feel like they are lasting forever to the victim, who might withdraw from a school's social life or skip school altogether. Targets may also change how they behave with friends, family and teachers, making home life and progress in class much harder.

Mild cases of bullying can have health effects, too, leading to sleeplessness, depression, poor health and even hair loss. It is hard to measure this effect, as most children who begin to skip school prefer to say they feel ill than to admit what is actually wrong.

▶ *Targets of bullying may want to skip school to escape being upset by the bullies.*

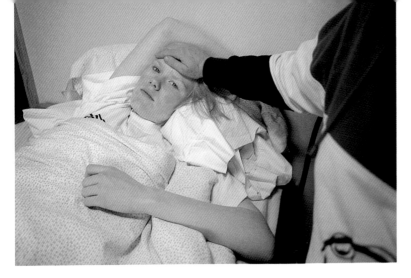

◀ *Children can fake being ill to avoid facing bullies at school – and they may actually become ill because of their feelings of stress and anxiety.*

Some people argue that a little bullying can have a positive effect on a child, as he or she learns how to deal with the problem and grows stronger as a result. There is no strong scientific evidence to support this claim. Those who do believe it may be talking about coping with less challenging behaviours, such as playful teasing among equals, than actual bullying.

Some adults believe that teachers and school counsellors can get too involved. They think that children must cope with some hard experiences and learn to trust themselves, rather than running for help all the time. They say that people have to learn how to be independent, and not always rely on the authorities. But such a response is not useful when a child is really under serious attack by bullies.

'Being bullied is not just an unpleasant rite of passage through childhood. It's a public health problem that merits attention. People who were bullied as children are more likely to suffer from depression and low self-esteem well into adulthood, and the bullies themselves are more likely to engage in criminal behavior later in life.'

Duane Alexander, director of the National Institute of Child Health and Human Development, Bethesda, Maryland, USA

Severe cases

Severe cases of bullying can be harmful to a child's development. Beyond missing school, victims of bullying may avoid contact with other children, which slows down the development of their social skills. They may find their teen years more difficult and frightening than most teenagers do. There may be more times in their adult lives when they will be reminded of feeling scared and ashamed.

In the worst cases, victims of bullying may come to believe that they are as worthless as their bully tells them they are. The experience of being hurt in public, and of others doing nothing to help, reinforces the sense that everyone hates you. It is hard to realize that others often may want to help, but are too scared to do anything. Children may be tempted to commit suicide as a result of being treated in this way.

▶ *Targets tend to become withdrawn and depressed, unable to share their problems.*

> **FACT:**
> Suicide as a result of bullying is most common in the age range 12-18. Girls are roughly four times more likely to attempt suicide than boys, but boys are more likely to do it secretively. As a result, more boys than girls die from suicide attempts. According to the American Center for Disease Control, roughly 20 per cent of high school students consider suicide as a serious option each year.
> *Canadian Institute of Child Health, 1995*

Where children are driven to despair, they may decide to take terrible revenge on the bully – and on people they think should have helped. In Littleton, Colorado, in 1999, Eric Harris and Dylan Klebold – both boys with a history of being teased and excluded at the High School – took guns there and killed 12 pupils and one teacher, as well as injuring others. They then killed themselves. The note of explanation they left blamed the whole school for the pain they had suffered.

Most people who suffer serious bullying as children are able to leave the experience behind them as they grow up. But there are some children who feel trapped by those experiences. It is hard to be sure how much is due to the bullying itself. Some may be due to emotional problems suffered around the time they were bullied, and some may have nothing to do with bullying at all. But there is no doubt that serious abuse as a child can have a bad effect in later life.

weblinks

For more information about the Columbine shootings, go to www.waylinks.co.uk/ series/why/bully

▼ *Eric Harris (below) and Dylan Klebold took 'revenge' for being bullied by shooting classmates and teachers at Columbine High School, Colorado in April 1999. In the main picture three children mourn the victims during a prayer vigil held in Denver, Colorado.*

5. How are bullies stopped?

What can targets do?

There are five main ways for a target to respond to a bully – they are described in the next four pages. None is guaranteed to succeed in all cases. The response that bullies usually look for is an emotional outburst, a 'proof' that the target has taken their attack seriously. Emotional responses satisfy the bully's aim – they show that the bully has found a spot where they are stronger than their target.

weblinks

For more information about talking to adults about bullying, go to www.waylinks.co.uk/ series/why/bully

Fighting back

At one time, it was common for parents to advise their children to stand up to bullies. But a bully rarely picks on someone who might be a serious opponent. Fighting back against all the odds is pointless. Just occasionally, a target has surprised a bully with an unexpected, painful response, and ended the bullying, but this approach is not recommended. The consequences are very unpredictable, and can result in the victim being punished by teachers – bullies are normally better at hiding their bad behaviour than other people.

▼ *Bullies pick on people who are less powerful than them – so fighting back is not usually the best option.*

Sometimes it helps to have other people around to stop a person from reacting angrily, and perhaps getting themselves into trouble.

Verbal come-backs are not much easier. Adults sometimes suggest clever things to say, but unless they feel natural and are said confidently, they can make the bullying worse. In cases of verbal teasing and indirect bullying, it can be difficult to know who is behind it and how to react.

Divert and distract

It is sometimes possible to turn a bully's attention to something else, especially when bullying arises out of boredom. Anything which interrupts the bully's plan can be enough to change the situation. It can even be quite easy to make a friend of them, if the target is calm and thinks carefully about how to win the bully's respect without being led into bad behaviour. But bullies can collect a set of 'followers' who support them in order to escape being picked on themselves. So it may be a bad solution to make friends – the target may end up having to bully others, or do other things that are wrong, to stay safe. In more serious cases, befriending is simply not an option for the target.

What can targets do?

Ignore

Refusing to react is a powerful response to verbal bullying. Bullies only look silly calling someone names when to everyone else that person seems relaxed or just bored. It is a hard act to keep up when you feel upset inside, especially if you have to say something to make things seem natural. It only works if the target can keep it up patiently, and for long enough for the bully to move on – it can take a week or more.

> 'We think of zero tolerance as the school's way of showing kids how we will not tolerate that kind of behavior, but this is a mere tactic to punish; it's retribution. We focus on the act and we forget the motives, and by doing that we may actually increase a kid's risk for future behavior problems, and at least the kid's alienation from school.'
>
> *Jaana Juvonen, professor, University of California at Berkeley*

To help stay calm, the target should try to think of what causes a bully to behave like this. Is the bully honestly criticizing me, or are they really rejecting something about themselves? Does everyone else hate me, or are they just too scared to do what's right? The point to hold onto is that you **never** deserve to be attacked. The hatred is not about you – it is driven by the bully's own problems, and by other people's fear of the bully.

◀ *Except in emergencies, running away from a bully is a bad solution – bullies see this as proof that the target is scared.*

Escape

Some targets try to slip away from a bully as soon as possible, and to avoid places where they are likely to meet them. This can help you in a serious situation, but may not work well over time. Escape isn't always possible, and bullies can enjoy trying to trap you. It may also encourage them to think of you as an easy target.

▲ *Taking problems to an adult may feel like 'cheating', but it is nothing to be ashamed of. It is normally the most effective way of dealing with a bully.*

Seek help

No-one wants to be a 'tell tale'. And it is often hard to admit that you cannot stand up for yourself, even though the odds are against you. But seeking help in a crisis is nothing to be ashamed of.

A friend or classmate can be the first people you ask for help. In serious cases, it might be better to go straight to an adult. Either way, make sure you are in control of what happens next. Be careful whom you tell. Pick someone you trust to respect your wishes. Make sure they understand that they need your permission before they do anything about what you have told them. Then talk it over and see if you agree with what they suggest.

Of all the five responses detailed here, telling an adult has been shown to be most effective.

What can peers do?

It is far more common to see someone being bullied than to be involved directly in an attack. Most of us wish we had the courage to help someone who is being badly treated. But few of us take the risk of getting involved. It is a real risk, especially when the target has

been made unpopular. For children, supporting an unpopular person is a very brave decision. But there are other options for witnesses to bullying.

▲ *Where bullying is a big problem, teachers can help schoolchildren form anti-bullying clubs or coalitions where problems can be aired and possible solutions discussed.*

• Ignoring: the first small step is to make sure the bully does not think that you agree with what they are doing.
• Disapproving: the next stage is to suggest to them that they stop it – to let them know that you think they are wrong.
• Defending: actively protecting the victim puts you in the firing line. Think about it carefully.
• Forming coalitions: this is less risky than defending someone on your own. Witnesses can band together to help a person, agreeing to keep an eye out for them.
• Reporting: the victim is often trapped by their reluctance to tell a teacher. Bystanders don't have to be.

weblinks▶

For more information about starting a project on bullying in your school, go to www.waylinks.co.uk/series/why/bully

The best approach will vary from case to case. Reporting can get results, but helping each other deal with bullies may have a longer-lasting and happier outcome. Some schools will help pupils launch a campaign against bullying or hold a survey to find out what people think. You could ask a student leader to talk to the head teacher about the idea.

▼ It takes a lot of courage for a witness to stand up to a bully and tell them that they are in the wrong – it may make the witness unpopular with the bully and, as a result, the next target.

FACT

A Canadian research project in 1995 filmed playground behaviour and studied it for bullying incidents. The research wanted to observe how witnesses behave. It found that, on average, four people witnessed each act of bullying recorded. About 75 per cent of the time, witnesses either encouraged the bully or did nothing - around 25 per cent of the time, they helped the victim.

What can adults do?

Teachers and school counsellors can do several things to help stop bullying. The approach that most parents of victims demand is punishment for the bully – a sort of revenge for the harm done to their own child. Until quite recently, most schools would have punished a bully, if caught, simply for breaking school rules.

In the USA and other English-speaking countries, a policy of zero tolerance of bullying is the latest version of this approach. It can be combined with a bully court, where a jury of pupils decides on cases and agrees punishments. Others argue that punishment is not a good solution. They note that it often provokes the bully to more cruelty, only better hidden, and into using nastier threats against people for telling.

▲ Adults need to think carefully about how to deal with bullying. Here a British politician, David Blunkett, is talking to three children about their experience of bullying at school.

case study · case study · case study · case study · case study

'When I was at the primary school, children bigger than me liked to bully me. In 1994 I was in grade 1 and a big boy liked to take my bread and cool drink. That boy left the school in grade 7. I was happy because the guy was not at the school any more, but … there were still boys who bullied me. I told the teacher about that, she warned them, but after school they bullied me again. I told the teacher that they [did not] want to stop bullying me. She gave them a last warning and they left me alone. I think all you have to do if someone bullies you is to tell someone bigger.'

Cederick, aged 14, South Africa

One successful alternative is called 'shared concern', invented in Sweden by bullying expert Anatol Pikas. The bully or bullies are made to attend a series of meetings, in which they are confronted with their victim's pain and encouraged to think about what they have been doing. This approach results in roughly two out of three bullies saying they are sorry for their behaviour, or at least changing the way they behave.

Adults also need to provide the right support for victims of bullying. Adults can help victims think about how they were targeted, and how they can develop skills to make them less easy to bully. They can also help classmates to come together to build support groups. But they also need to act carefully. Children sometimes will make up stories, or even provoke people into breaking rules just to get them into trouble. In every case, adults should think calmly about the best solution.

◄ *This American beauty queen, Miss America 2003 Erika Harold, was a victim of bullying at school. She is seen arguing for new laws against bullying at a public meeting in Connecticut.*

45

GLOSSARY

Aggressive
Tending to seek conflict and violence.

Anti-social
Harmful to the well-being of a community.

Assertive
Tending to stand up for oneself.

Befriending
Taking care of someone who needs help and support.

Coalition
A group formed to achieve a goal.

Co-ed
Short for co-educational, meaning a school where boys and girls are taught together.

Community
A group of people living together as a unit.

Counsellor
A person trained to help others with their problems.

Criticize
To find fault with.

Depression
Feeling deeply sad, especially about one's own life.

Distract/divert
Turn attention away from something.

DNA
Deoxyribonucleic acid – the material that makes up the chromosomes in our bodies which contain the genetic code that makes each individual what they are.

Employee
A person who is paid to work for someone else.

Environment
The surroundings which affect a person or other living thing.

Ethos
The customs and 'character' of a person or place.

Exclude
To leave someone out of an activity deliberately.

Genes
The biological 'instructions' passed from parent to offspring that determine how that offspring will look and develop.

Grade
A standard American naming system for school years.

Hazing
Customs and initiation ceremonies that are designed to embarrass and belittle new members of a group.

Identity
An idea of the self as a single whole.

Interact
To act on each other; people in a group interact with one another.

Intervene
To get involved with, or come between, often in order to try to change a situation.

Mentor
A person who advises and tutors another.

Nurture
To nourish and bring up, e.g. a child.

Offspring
A biological word for babies.

Peers
Friends, and other people of similar age and experience.

Physical
To do with the body as opposed to the mind.

Poverty
Having too little money to live a healthy life.

Primates
The set of mammals which includes lemurs, monkeys, apes and humans.

Rite of passage
An event of particular significance in a person's life.

Role model
An inspiring person who serves as a model for other people.

Self-esteem
How you rate yourself as a person – having low self-esteem means that you do not think very highly of yourself.

Statistics
Numbers which communicate the results of research.

Status
Position or rank within a group or a society as a whole.

Suicide
Ending your own life on purpose.

Survey
A systematic collection of information from a wide range of sources.

Taunt
To mock or jeer at someone.

Threat
An indication of danger.

Traumatize
To cause injury.

Unpredictable
Hard to predict.

Verbal
Using words, especially spoken words.

Victimize
To pick on and overpower someone so that they become your victim.

Vulnerable
Sensitive, or open to attack.

Zero tolerance
A style of discipline focusing on sharp punishment for rule breakers, not accepting excuses.

FURTHER INFORMATION

BOOKS TO READ

For children
Bullies, Big Mouths & So-called Best Friends by Jenny Alexander (Hodder Children's Books, 2003) – tips to help you deal with the people in your life who are making you miserable.
Cliques, Phonies and Other Baloney by Trevor Romain (Free Spirit Publishing, 1998) – fun ways to think about friends, exclusion from groups, and being trapped in a group.
How to Handle Bullies, Teasers and Other Meanies by Kate Cohen-Posey (Rainbow Books, 1995) – packed with suggestions to help deal with verbal bullying.

For teachers and parents:
The Bully-Free Classroom by Allan L Beane (Free Spirit Publishing, 1999) – practical tips and handout materials from an experienced practitioner.
New Perspectives on Bullying by Ken Rigby (Jessica Kingsley Publishers, 2002) – the most comprehensive evidence-based overview available.
Stop The Bullying: A Handbook for Schools by Ken Rigby (Jessica Kingsley Publishers, 2001) – another helpful handbook about school bullying.
What To Do When Kids Are Mean To Your Child by Elin McCoy (Reader's Digest, 1997) – simple strategies for parents to work through, with the kids and alone!

ORGANIZATIONS

UK
Anti-bullying campaign: tel 020 7378 1446

Childline: tel 0800 1111
Support for any problems a child is coping with.

Kidscape: tel 020 7730 3300
Charity with great advice and resources for kids on bullying.

Australia
Kids Helpline (Australia): tel 1800 55 1800

WEBSITES
For websites that are relevant to this book, go to www.waylinks.co.uk/series/why/bully

INDEX